I Am...
American History

100 Mini Posters
of Famous People
in American History!

Sunflower
education

Exceptional Books for Teachers and Parents™

A Great Way to Teach American History!

I Am American History! is a unique collection of 100 mini posters that humanize historical figures. First-person statements include intriguing details that bring figures to life. Quotations inspire and provoke thought. Includes many creative suggestions for active classroom use.

100 Mini Posters
Each poster includes major accomplishments, quotation, and
"here's something you may not know about me" detail.
Grades 4 and up.

Please feel free to photocopy the posters in this book within reason. Sunflower Education grants teachers permission to photocopy posters from this book for educational use. This permission is granted to individual teachers and not entire schools or school systems. Please send any permissions questions to permissions@SunflowerEducation.net.

Visit **SunflowerEducation.Net** for more great books!

Editorial   Sunflower Education

Design   Blue Agave Studio

Photography
Cover images, ©Lisa F. Young/Shutterstock Images LLC; ©iStockphoto LP
Interior book images, Wikimedia Commons

ISBN-13: 978-1-937166-09-0
ISBN-10: 1-937166-09-0
Copyright © 2011
Sunflower Education
All rights reserved.
Printed in the U.S.A.

Contents

To The Teacher 1

1. Abigail Adams
2. John Adams
3. John Quincy Adams
4. Susan B. Anthony
5. Neil Armstrong
6. Clara Barton
7. Alexander Graham Bell
8. William Bradford
9. John Brown
10. William Jennings Bryan
11. John C. Calhoun
12. Andrew Carnegie
13. Cesar Chavez
14. Henry Clay
15. Bill Clinton
16. Calvin Coolidge
17. James Fenimore Cooper
18. Francisco Vasquez de Coronado
19. Charles Coughlin
20. George Custer
21. Jefferson Davis
22. Jack Dempsey
23. Dorothea Dix
24. Frederick Douglass
25. W.E.B. Du Bois
26. Amelia Earhart
27. Thomas Edison
28. Albert Einstein
29. Dwight D. Eisenhower
30. Ralph Waldo Emerson
31. Enrico Fermi
32. F. Scott Fitzgerald
33. Stephen Foster
34. Benjamin Franklin
35. Betty Friedan
36. William Lloyd Garrison
37. Ulysses S. Grant
38. Alexander Hamilton
39. Ernest Hemingway
40. Herbert Hoover
41. Andrew Jackson
42. Thomas Jefferson
43. John Paul Jones
44. Helen Keller
45. Florence Kelley
46. John F. Kennedy
47. Martin Luther King, Jr.
48. Robert E. Lee
49. Meriwether Lewis
50. Sinclair Lewis

51.	Abraham Lincoln	**76.**	Upton Sinclair
52.	Charles Lindbergh	**77.**	Sitting Bull
53.	Benjamin Lundy	**78.**	John Smith
54.	James Madison	**79.**	Squanto
55.	Horace Mann	**80.**	Elizabeth Cady Stanton
56.	John Marshall	**81.**	Harriet Beecher Stowe
57.	Thurgood Marshall	**82.**	William Graham Sumner
58.	Cyrus McCormick	**83.**	William Howard Taft
59.	James Monroe	**84.**	Ida Tarbell
60.	J. P. Morgan	**85.**	Zachary Taylor
61.	Samuel F. B. Morse	**86.**	Henry David Thoreau
62.	Annie Oakley	**87.**	Bill Tilden
63.	Barack Obama	**88.**	Harry S. Truman
64.	Sandra Day O'Connor	**89.**	Frederick Jackson Turner
65.	Thomas Paine	**90.**	Mark Twain
66.	Rosa Parks	**91.**	Cornelius Vanderbilt
67.	Frances Perkins	**92.**	Amerigo Vespucci
68.	Ronald Reagan	**93.**	George Washington
69.	Sally Ride	**94.**	Booker T. Washington
70.	Jackie Robinson	**95.**	Eli Whitney
71.	John D. Rockefeller	**96.**	Walt Whitman
72.	Eleanor Roosevelt	**97.**	Woodrow Wilson
73.	Franklin D. Roosevelt	**98.**	Orville Wright
74.	Sacagawea	**99.**	Wilber Wright
75.	Dred Scott	**100.**	Brigham Young

To the Teacher

Posters are a lot more important than many teachers and homeschoolers think. The truth is that posters are pedagogical powerhouses!

The Benefits of Posters

For 50 years, scientific research has consistently established the presence of educational posters as a major classroom asset. "By simply selecting and hanging aesthetically pleasing posters in your classroom," notes the University of Binghamton's Thomas O'Brien, "you are increasing the visual interests of your classroom. In turn, this creates a pleasant environment likely to encourage more positive student attitudes and behaviors."

But that's only the beginning. The presence of posters is a strong indicator that the environment is for *learning*. Let's face it: kids' minds wander off topic and their eyes off of what they are doing. "Knowing and anticipating this phenomenon," O'Brien continues, "allows you to strategically prepare for your students' wandering minds. Great posters attract and retain student attention. Visually stimulating posters that are aligned with the content of the unit can be an ideal method to providing students with germane targets for their mental escapes."

What Makes *I Am American History!* Posters Special

Historical figures are often nothing but abstract names in students' minds. The *I Am American History!* posters help humanize the figures, to make them seem more like real people. Each poster does so in four ways:

- **First Person** The text is not about the person, it is *by* the person.
- **An Intimate Portrait** The image for each historical figure is the most modern-looking one available.
- **Quotation** The prominent quotation works like a speech bubble to help animate the individual.
- **Here's Something You May Not Know About Me** Lighthearted information about the figure makes them an accessible "real person" in students minds.

How to Use the Posters in This Book

The posters in *I Am American History!* are designed to support the study of American history. You can maximize their impact by employing certain techniques.

- **Rotate the Posters** Make sure you change the posters to align with current study units.
- **Do Not Rotate Some Posters** Leave some posters permanently in place. Over time, this consistency is intellectually comforting to some students and promotes memorization.
- **Draw Attention to and Discuss the Posters** Consider the posters together as a class. Tell students that time spent reading them is not wasted.
- **Make a Person of the Week Spot on a Classroom Wall** Once a week, choose one historical figure on which to focus. Consider letting a student select the person as a reward. Of course, you can make it "People of the Week" and consider multiple historical figures.
- **Make Bulletin Board Displays** You can use the posters as the basis of bulletin board displays. See "Suggested Groupings."

- **Time Lines** Use the posters as entries on bulletin board or wall-mounted time lines.
- **Build a People Pyramid** As students learn about an individual, attach the poster near the bottom of a classroom wall. Make one row, then, above it, a slightly smaller row. Continue the process until, at the end of the year, the pyramid is complete.
- **Hold a Scavenger Hunt** With many posters up, challenge students to locate items on a scavenger hunt. For example, an author, an astronaut, a general, the person who stated that "the first duty of society is justice," and so on.
- **Make the Classroom a Giant Concept Map** With many posters up, challenge students to connect various posters with string and to explain the connections (e.g., figures of the Civil War).
- **Use as Openers and Closers for Units of Study** Discuss appropriate individuals as a way to introduce and humanize units of study. Review the major ideas of units of study by connecting them to individuals.
- **Discuss Quotations** The quotations on the posters, taken together, are a remarkable collection of insight and advice from some of the greatest Americans.
- **Build Vocabulary** Many of the quotations and texts include words that may be unfamiliar to students. Seize the opportunity to expand students' vocabulary using the context of both language and history (e.g., William Lloyd Garrison's refusal to *equivocate* in his opposition to slavery).

Suggested Groupings

The mini posters of *I Am American History!* make excellent material for bulletin boards. The table provides several ideas.

Visit SunflowerEducation.net for additional groupings, free downloads of bulletin board labels, time line dates, and more!

Abolitionists	9. John Brown; 36. William Lloyd Garrison; 53. Benjamin Lundy; 81. Harriet Beecher Stowe
Authors	17. James Fenimore Cooper; 30. Ralph Waldo Emerson; 32. F. Scott Fitzgerald; 39. Ernest Hemingway; 44. Helen Keller; 50. Sinclair Lewis; 65. Thomas Paine; 76. Upton Sinclair; 81. Harriet Beecher Stowe; 82. William Graham Sumner; 84. Ida Tarbell; 86. Henry David Thoreau; 89. Frederick Jackson Turner; 90. Mark Twain; 94. Booker T. Washington; 96. Walt Whitman
Aviators	26. Amelia Earhart; 52. Charles Lindbergh; 97. Orville Wright; 98. Wilbur Wright
Businessmen	12. Andrew Carnegie; 60. J.P. Morgan; 71. John D. Rockefeller; 91. Cornelius Vanderbilt
Celebrities	22. Jack Dempsey; 33. Stephen Foster; 62. Annie Oakley; 70. Jackie Robinson; 87. Bill Tilden

Civil Rights Leaders	4. Susan B. Anthony; 13. Cesar Chavez; 23. Dorothea Dix; 24. Frederick Douglass; 25. W.E.B. Du Bois; 35. Betty Friedan; 45. Florence Kelley; 47. Martin Luther King, Jr.; 67. Frances Perkins; 72. Eleanor Roosevelt; 80. Elizabeth Cady Stanton
Explorers	5. Neil Armstrong; 18. Francisco Vasquez de Coronado; 49. Meriwether Lewis; 69. Sally Ride; 92. Amerigo Vespucci
Famous Native Americans	74. Sacagawea; 77. Sitting Bull; 79. Squanto
Founders	2. John Adams; 34. Benjamin Franklin; 38. Alexander Hamilton; 42. Thomas Jefferson; 54. James Madison; 93. George Washington
Great Women	1. Abigail Adams; 4. Susan B. Anthony; 6. Clara Barton; 23. Dorothea Dix; 26. Amelia Earhart; 35. Betty Friedan; 44. Helen Keller; 45. Florence Kelley; 62. Annie Oakley; 64. Sandra Day O'Connor; 66. Rosa Parks; 67. Frances Perkins; 69. Sally Ride; 72. Eleanor Roosevelt; 74. Sacagawea; 80. Elizabeth Cady Stanton; 81. Harriet Beecher Stowe; 84. Ida Tarbell
Inventors	7. Alexander Graham Bell; 27. Thomas Edison; 58. Cyrus McCormick; 61. Samuel F. B. Morse; 95. Eli Whitney
Leaders	8. William Bradford; 10. William Jennings Bryan; 11. John C. Calhoun; 14. Henry Clay; 38. Alexander Hamilton; 55. Horace Mann
Leaders of American Groups	21. Jefferson Davis; 77. Sitting Bull; 78. John Smith; 100. Brigham Young
Military Leaders	20. George Custer; 37. Ulysses S. Grant; 43. John Paul Jones; 48. Robert E. Lee; 77. Sitting Bull; 85. Zachary Taylor; 93. George Washington
Presidents	2. John Adams; 3. John Quincy Adams; 15. Bill Clinton; 16. Calvin Coolidge; 29. Dwight D. Eisenhower; 37. Ulysses S. Grant; 40. Herbert Hoover; 41. Andrew Jackson; 42. Thomas Jefferson; 46. John F. Kennedy; 51. Abraham Lincoln; 54. James Madison; 59. James Monroe; 63. Barack Obama; 68. Ronald Reagan; 73. Franklin D. Roosevelt; 83. William Howard Taft; 85. Zachary Taylor; 88. Harry S. Truman; 93. George Washington; 99. Woodrow Wilson
Religious Figures	19. Charles Coughlin; 100. Brigham Young
Scientists	28. Albert Einstein; 31. Enrico Fermi
Supreme Court Justices	56. John Marshall; 57. Thurgood Marshall; 64. Sandra Day O'Connor

I Am... Abigail Adams 1744–1818

first lady

"If we mean to have heroes, statesmen and philosophers, we should have learned women."

I was the second first lady of the United States. My husband was John Adams, the Founder and president. He sought my advice on a wide variety of matters. I voiced strong support for the rights of women. Here's something you may not know about me: as a child, I was too sick to attend school, but that didn't stop me from getting an education!

I Am.... John Adams

1735–1826

founder

"A government of laws, and not of men."

I was the second president of the United States—and the first one to live in the White House! As a Founder, I was instrumental in stirring up anti-British sentiment. After the Revolution, though, I helped negotiate the peace. Here's something you may not know about me: I was very proud of the fact that my ancestors were among the first Puritans in America!

I Am...
John Quincy Adams
1767–1848

president

"If your actions inspire others to dream more, learn more, do more and become more, you are a leader."

I was John Adams' son and the sixth president of the United States. Earlier, I had served as an active and successful secretary of state. As president, I wanted to modernize the economy. Here's something you may not know about me: I took the oath of office on a book of laws instead of on a Bible because I believed in separation of church and state!

I Am... Susan B. Anthony
1820–1906

women's rights activist

"Men their rights and nothing more; women their rights and nothing less."

I devoted myself to promoting the rights of American women. I worked tirelessly for women's suffrage and for equal educational, property, and marriage rights. Earlier, I was active in the temperance and abolition movements. Here's something you may not know about me: I was the first woman to appear on a U.S. coin—the Susan B. Anthony dollar!

I Am... Neil Armstrong b. 1930

"That's one small step for man, one giant leap for mankind."

astronaut

I was the first person to set foot on the moon! In 1969, I walked on the moon with fellow astronaut Buzz Aldrin. We, along with Michael Collins, were the crew of the Apollo 11 mission. Together, we planted an American flag on the moon. Here's something you may not know about me: I got my pilot's license at age 15—before I got my driver's license!

I Am... Clara Barton 1821–1912

"If I can't be a soldier, I'll help soldiers."

nurse

I nursed wounded soldiers during the Civil War. People called me the "Angel of the Battlefield." Later, I founded the American Red Cross. I organized the relief efforts for several natural disasters. Here's something you may not know about me: I helped my first patient, my injured brother, when I was only 11 years old!

I Am...
Alexander Graham Bell
1847–1922

"When one door closes another door opens; but we often look...so regretfully upon the closed door, that we do not see the ones which open for us."

inventor

I invented the telephone! My very helpful assistant was Thomas Watson. We first succeeded in transmitting the human voice in 1876. Here's something you may not know about me: after I invented the telephone, I went on to create a type of metal detector, a device for locating icebergs, and kites that were used to lift people into the air!

I Am... William Bradford
1590 – 1657

governor

"As one small candle may light a thousand, so the light here kindled hath shone unto many, yea in some sort to our whole nation."

I was elected 30 times to be governor of Plymouth. I led Plymouth through crises like drought, crop failures, and financial problems. My book *Of Plimouth Plantation* provides historians with a great deal of information about our colony. Here's something you may not know about me: I organized the first Thanksgiving!

I Am... John Brown 1800-1859

abolitionist

"Caution, Sir! I am eternally tired of hearing that word ....It is nothing but the word of cowardice!"

I was an abolitionist who believed that slavery should be ended immediately. My raid on Harper's Ferry was actually a raid on an armory. I was going to use the weapons to arm the slaves and incite a mass revolt. However, I was caught and hanged. Here's something you may not know about me: in my youth, I helped escaped slaves make it into Canada!

I Am...
William Jennings Bryan
1860–1925

"My place in history will depend on what I can do for the people and not on what the people can do for me."

statesman

I was a leading politician and orator who ran for president three times. The popular positions I took against monied interests earned me the nickname "The Commoner." Here's something you may not know about me: in the days before radio and television, public speaking was a popular attraction, and I was one of the most popular speakers of all!

I Am... John C. Calhoun
1782–1850

statesman

"Government has within it a tendency to abuse its powers."

I was a major figure in American politics in the first half of the 1800s. I served as vice president to both Andrew Jackson and John Quincy Adams. A true southerner from South Carolina, I was an outspoken supporter of states' rights. Here's something you may not know about me: my nickname was "The Cast-Iron Man"!

I Am...
Andrew Carnegie
1835–1919

industrialist

"No man can become rich without himself enriching others."

I founded the Carnegie Steel Company, the largest steel company in the world, and became amazingly wealthy. I used my fortune to fund nearly 3,000 libraries, construct Carnegie Hall in New York, and fund other good causes. Here's something you may not know about me: as a teenager, I worked in a cotton mill and as a telegraph operator!

12

I Am...
Cesar Chavez
1927–1993

civil rights activist

"You cannot oppress the people who are not afraid anymore."

I worked to protect Mexican American farm workers from unfair treatment. My techniques to improve working conditions included strikes and boycotts. I founded the United Farm Workers of America. Here's something you may not know about me: I served in the Navy, and today there is a ship named after me!

I Am... Henry Clay
1777–1852

statesman

"I would rather be right than president."

I was a leading figure in American government. I represented Kentucky in both houses of Congress. As the "Great Compromiser," I played a key role in crafting the Missouri Compromise and the Compromise of 1850. Here's something you may not know about me: counties, cities, schools, dormitories, streets, and even a submarine are named for me!

I Am...
Bill Clinton
b. 1946

"We cannot build our own future without helping others to build theirs."

president

I was the president of the United States from 1993 to 2001. Earlier, I served as governor of Arkansas. As president, I wanted to focus on domestic issues. During my second term I was impeached but found not guilty. Here's something you may not know about me: I played the saxophone in high school—and, as a presidential candidate, on TV!

I Am...
Calvin Coolidge
1872–1933

"The chief business of the American people is business."

president

© 2011 Sunflower Education   Sunflower.Education.net

I was president during the Roaring Twenties, but I was very serious and somewhat shy. My nickname was "Silent Cal." I advocated "constructive economy," and I worked to help American businesses at home and overseas. Here's something you may not know about me: I was a farm boy who grew up doing chores!

I Am...
James Fenimore Cooper
1789–1851

author

"Should we distrust the man because his manners are not our manners, and that his skin is dark?"

I wrote a series of novels that were the first important works of fiction about the American frontier. The most famous is *The Last of the Mohicans*. They are exciting stories about a woodsman named Natty Bumppo. Here's something you may not know about me: I loved pranks, and once taught a donkey to sit in my professor's chair!

I Am...
Francisco Vasquez de Coronado 1510(?)-1554

"Neither gold nor silver nor any trace of either was found."

explorer

I explored northern Mexico and the American Southwest looking for the Seven Cities of Cibola. Legend told of these cities rich in gold, silver, and jewels. I journeyed as far as Kansas looking for riches, but I never found them. Here's something you may not know about me: I thought the tortillas made by the Zuni people were the best I ever had!

I Am...
Charles Coughlin
1891–1979

radio commentator

"The laboring and agricultural classes of America are forced to work for less than a living wage while the owners of industry boastfully proclaim that their profits are increasing."

I was a Catholic priest who gained a huge following through my radio show in the 1930s. Like pundits today, I commented on the political, economic, and social issues of the time. My anti-Semitic and pro-fascist beliefs led to me being forced off the air. Here's something you may not know about me: about one third of Americans listened to my radio show!

19

© 2011 Sunflower Education   SunflowerEducation.net

I Am... George Custer
1839–1876

general

"I would be willing, yes glad, to see a battle every day during my life."

During the Civil War, I fought on the Union side and earned a reputation for boldness, bravery, and victory. I was promoted to major general. Later, I led the Army forces in the Battle of Little Bighorn, which saw the Seventh Cavalry defeated. Here's something you may not know about me: I was only 23 when I became the "Boy General"!

I Am... Jefferson Davis

1808–1889

confederate leader

"Never be haughty to the humble or humble to the haughty."

I was the president of the Confederate States of America. Interestingly, I earlier served in the U.S. Army and Senate. I even served as secretary of war under President Franklin Pierce. But I was a strong supporter of slavery and states' rights. Here's something you may not know about me: after the Civil War, I sold my plantation to one of my former slaves!

21

I Am... Dorothea Dix
1802–1887

social reformer

"In a world where there is so much to be done, I felt strongly impressed that there must be something for me to do."

I spent my life trying to improve conditions for prisoners and people with mental illnesses. I led the drive to create the first public mental health hospitals. Also, I served in the Civil War as Superintendent of Army Nurses. Here's something you may not know about me: I saw to it that nurses cared for wounded Confederate soldiers as well as Union soldiers!

I Am... Frederick Douglass 1817–1895

social reformer

"The soul that is within me no man can degrade."

I was born into slavery, but I escaped and worked against it for the rest of my life. I was an excellent orator who spoke of what freedom meant. My antislavery autobiography was a best seller. I founded an abolitionist newspaper, the *North Star*. Here's something you may not know about me: because I was born a slave, I didn't even know my own birthday!

I Am... W.E.B. DuBois
1868–1963

civil rights activist

"Believe in life! Always human beings will live and progress to greater, broader, and fuller life."

I was a historian, sociologist, and leading voice for racial equality. My book *The Souls of Black Folk* was a landmark study and discussion of African American life. I helped found the National Association for the Advancement of Colored People (NAACP). Here's something you may not know about me: I earned a doctorate from Harvard University!

I Am...
Amelia Earhart
1897 – 1937(?)

aviator

"You can do anything you decide to do. You can act to change and control your life...."

I broke many records and earned many awards. I was the first woman to fly across the Atlantic Ocean alone. In 1937, I disappeared over the Pacific Ocean while on a round-the-world flight. Here's something you may not know about me: I wanted so badly to learn how to fly, I worked at several jobs, including as a truck driver, to save up the money for flying lessons!

I Am...
Thomas Edison
1847–1931

inventor

"I have not failed. I've just found 10,000 ways that won't work."

I invented the light bulb! I also invented the phonograph, the motion picture camera, and more than a thousand other things! My research lab was located in Menlo Park, New Jersey, and I was called the "Wizard of Menlo Park." Here's something you may not know about me: I believed that "genius is one percent inspiration, ninety-nine percent perspiration"!

I Am...
Albert Einstein
1879–1955

scientist

"Imagination is more important than knowledge."

I am one of the most famous scientists who ever lived. I developed the theory of relativity and other important ideas. In 1921, I was awarded the Nobel Prize for physics. Here's something you may not know about me: my fascination with science began when my father showed me a magnetic compass when I was about five years old!

I Am...
Dwight D. Eisenhower
1890–1969

"Pessimism never won any battle."

president

I was the Supreme Commander of the Allied Forces in World War II and the 34th president of the United States. As president in the 1950s, I led a nation prosperous at home but confronting communism overseas. Here's something you may not know about me: my support was key to adding "under God" to the Pledge of Allegiance in 1954!

29

I Am...
Ralph Waldo Emerson
1803–1882

"Do not go where the path may lead, go instead where there is no path and leave a trail."

transcendentalist

I was a writer and speaker and leader of the Transcendentalist movement, which emphasized the divinity of all things and the importance of nature. I wrote "Self-Reliance" and many other essays and poems that are still revered today. Here's something you may not know about me: I grew up in poverty, but I didn't let that stop me!

I Am...
Enrico Fermi
1901–1954

"Ignorance is never better than knowledge."

scientist

I won the Nobel Prize in physics in 1938 and later worked on the Manhattan Project, which created the first atomic bomb. I designed the first nuclear reactor. Although I was born in Italy, I became an American citizen in 1944. Here's something you may not know about me: the element fermium and particles called fermions are named after me!

I Am...
F. Scott Fitzgerald
1896–1940

"Genius is the ability to put into effect what is on your mind."

author

I was a member of the Lost Generation of writers during the 1920s. Much of my work was about the contrast between youth and promise and old age and despair. My most famous novel, *The Great Gatsby*, explored relationships between wealth and morality. Here's something you may not know about me: I also wrote scripts for Hollywood movies!

I Am... Stephen Foster

1826–1864

composer

"Beautiful dreamer, wake unto me, Starlight and dewdrops are waiting for thee...."

I am known as the "Father of American Music" for writing songs such as "Camptown Races," "Oh! Susanna," and "Beautiful Dreamer." I also wrote "Old Folks at Home," which many people call "Swanee River." Here's something you may not know about me: I taught myself to play the clarinet...when I was six years old!

I Am... Benjamin Franklin
1706-1790

founder

"Either write something worth reading or do something worth writing."

I was one of the Founders and I convinced the French to support the American Revolution. I invented the lightning rod, bifocals, and the Franklin stove. My *Poor Richard's Almanack* was full of advice and sayings like "A penny saved is a penny earned." Here's something you may not know about me: I formed the first U.S. public library!

I Am... Betty Friedan
1921–2006

"A girl should not expect special privileges...but neither should she adjust to prejudice and discrimination."

feminist

I founded the National Organization for Women and wrote *The Feminine Mystique*. It examined the effects of limiting women's opportunities outside the household. Some people say I founded modern feminism. Here's something you may not know about me: my mom gave up her job as a journalist to raise her children; she inspired me to have my own career!

I Am...
William Lloyd Garrison
1805–1879

"I am in earnest—
I will not equivocate—
I will not excuse—
I will not retreat a
single inch—
AND I WILL BE HEARD!"

abolitionist

I founded the abolitionist newspaper *The Liberator*. In it, I called for immediate emancipation when other abolitionists called for a gradual end to slavery. After abolition, I worked for women's suffrage. Here's something you may not know about me: because of my stand, many people threatened my life, and I was almost lynched by a mob in Boston!

I Am... Ulysses S. Grant
1822–1885

president

> "I have never advocated war except as a means of peace."

I commanded the Union Army during the Civil War. I went on to serve two terms as president. Here's something you may not know about me: my real name was Hiram Ulysses Grant, and I was afraid that other boys would make fun of my initials spelling "HUG"—when my name was changed by mistake in some paperwork, I didn't say anything!

I Am...

Alexander Hamilton
1757–1804

founder

"I think the first duty of society is justice."

During the Revolutionary War, I was an aide-de-camp to George Washington. Later, I served as the first secretary of the treasury, and I helped establish the U.S. Mint and the first national bank. I wrote *The Federalist* with John Jay and James Madison. Here's something you may not know about me: as a child, I loved to read and write!

I Am... Ernest Hemingway 1899–1961

author

"All good books have one thing in common—they are truer than if they had really happened."

I won the Nobel Prize for literature. I also won a Pulitzer Prize. Some of my best-known novels are *A Farewell to Arms, The Sun Also Rises,* and *For Whom the Bell Tolls.* I was famous for a writing style that was plain and for a lifestyle that was masculine and adventurous. Here's something you may not know about me: as a boy, I played cello in the school orchestra!

I Am...
Herbert Hoover
1874 – 1964

president

"Children are our most valuable natural resource."

I was president when the Great Depression started. Many people blamed the hard economic times on me. Homeless people built tent cities they called "Hoovervilles." Here's something you may not know about me: as a young man, I worked pulling weeds, managing a laundry, delivering newspapers, and in a mine!

I Am... Andrew Jackson
1767–1845

president

"Any man worth his salt will stick up for what he believes right, but it takes a slightly better man to acknowledge... that he is in error."

I was the seventh president of the United States—but the first one born in a log cabin! I grew up on the frontier, and was popular with ordinary working people. As a military man, I fought Indians and became a general during the War of 1812. Here's something you may not know about me: my nickname was "Old Hickory" because I was so tough!

I Am... Thomas Jefferson

1743–1826

founder

"Do you want to know who you are? Don't ask. Act! Action will delineate and define you."

I wrote the Declaration of Independence and was the third president of the United States. As president, I approved the Louisiana Purchase, which more than doubled the size of the United States. I was also a diplomat and great thinker. Here's something you may not know about me: I was a farm boy who grew up hunting, fishing, and riding horses!

I Am... John Paul Jones
1747–1792

naval hero

"I have not yet begun to fight!"

I am the "Father of the American Navy." In the Revolutionary War, I captained a ship, the *Bonhomme Richard (Poor Richard)*, which I named in honor of Benjamin Franklin (who wrote *Poor Richard's Almanack*). Here's something you may not know about me: my quote above was my response to the captain of a British ship who demanded I surrender!

I Am...

Helen Keller

1880–1968

author

"All the world is full of suffering. It is also full of overcoming."

Due to an illness when I was 19 months old, I lost both my hearing and my sight. My teacher, Anne Sullivan, taught me how to speak sign language and to read Braille. I became the first deaf and blind person to earn a bachelor of arts. Here's something you may not know about me: I wrote 12 books, one of which is simply titled *Optimism!*

I Am...
Florence Kelley
1859–1932

civil rights activist

"There can be no pause in the agitation for full political power and responsibility until these are granted to all the women of the nation."

I fought against sweatshops and child labor and I fought for a minimum wage and women's suffrage. I ran the National Consumers League, which urged consumers to support businesses that treated workers fairly. Here's something you may not know about me: Secretary of Labor Frances Perkins called me "Explosive, hot-tempered....a smoking volcano"!

I Am...
John F. Kennedy
1917–1963

president

"And so, my fellow Americans, ask not what your country can do for you; ask what you can do for your country."

In 1960, I became the youngest president ever elected. I was also the first president born in the 20th century. I started the Peace Corps and was a firm advocate of civil rights. My presidency was cut short by an assassin in 1963. Here's something you may not know about me: in high school, I was voted "most likely to succeed"!

46

I Am...
Martin Luther King, Jr.
1929–1968

civil rights activist

"**Darkness cannot drive out darkness; only light can do that. Hate cannot drive out hate; only love can do that.**"

I spent my life working to achieve equal rights for African Americans through nonviolent protests. I led the Montgomery bus boycott and gave the famous "I Have a Dream" speech in Washington, D.C. I was assassinated in 1968. Here's something you may not know about me: I started college when I was only 15 years old!

I Am... Robert E. Lee
1807–1870

"Do your duty in all things. You cannot do more, you should never wish to do less."

general

I led the Confederate Army during the Civil War. Even though I fought for the South, I disliked slavery and thought the war was a bad idea. I only fought for the South because I loved my home of Virginia. Here's something you may not know about me: before the Civil War, I was actually friends with Ulysses S. Grant!

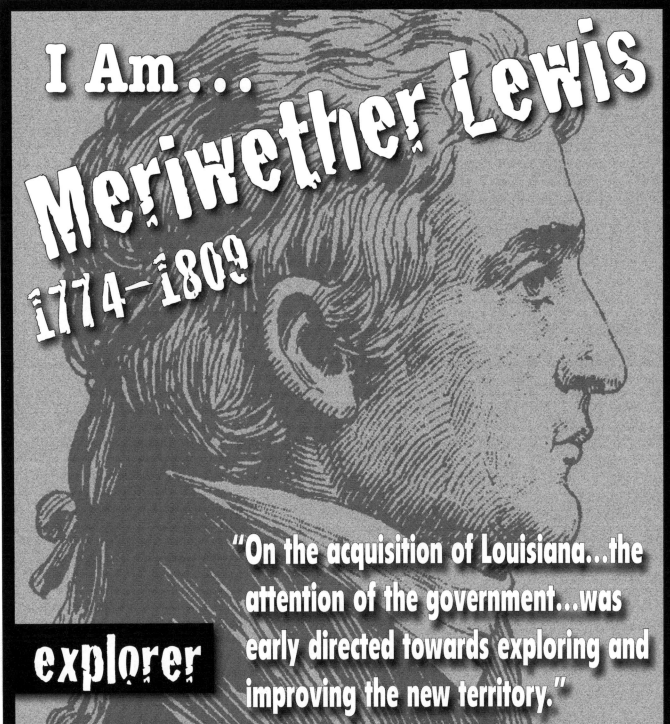

I Am... Meriwether Lewis

1774-1809

explorer

"On the acquisition of Louisiana...the attention of the government...was early directed towards exploring and improving the new territory."

I was entrusted by Thomas Jefferson to explore the Louisiana Purchase and Oregon region. With my friend William Clark, I led the famous Lewis and Clark Expedition from 1804 to 1806. Here's something you may not know about me: I developed a keen interest in natural history as a boy, so it is appropriate that a plant, a fish, and a bird are all named for me!

I Am... Sinclair Lewis 1885–1951

author

"Intellectually I know that America is no better than any other country; emotionally I know she is better than every country."

I was the first American to be awarded the Nobel Prize for literature. My most famous works are *Main Street*, *Babitt*, and *It Can't Happen Here*. I was a keen observer of people and created compelling characters. Much of my work satirizes American life. Here's something you may not know about me: as a boy, I was tall and skinny and felt socially awkward!

I Am... Abraham Lincoln
1809–1865

president

"Government of the people, by the people, for the people...."

I was president during the Civil War. My Emancipation Proclamation led to the end of slavery. Tragically, I was assassinated just days after the defeat of the Confederacy. Had I lived, I might have ensured the South was treated better after the war. Here's something you may not know about me: in Illinois, I was a well-respected local wrestler!

51

I Am...
Charles Lindbergh
1902–1974

"I don't believe in taking foolish chances. But nothing can be accomplished by not taking a chance at all."

aviator

I was a pioneering aviator, and the first modern international celebrity. My nonstop solo flight across the Atlantic in 1927 was the first ever, and it made me world famous. The name of my airplane was the *Spirit of St. Louis*. Here's something you may not know about me: my family moved around so much, I never went to any one school for more than a year!

I Am...
Benjamin Lundy
1789 – 1839

"Slavery endangers our liberties."

abolitionist

I was a Quaker who spent my life working against slavery. I gave speeches and wrote books in favor of abolition. Often I was harassed and beaten for my efforts, and once a mob burned down my house. Here's something you may not know about me: you can visit my home—it's a National Historic Landmark in Mount Pleasant, Ohio!

I Am.... James Madison
1751–1836

"All men having power ought to be distrusted to a certain degree."

founder

I was the fourth president of the United States. I am revered as the "Father of the Constitution" because of my work creating that document— and our government. With Alexander Hamilton and John Jay, I wrote *The Federalist*. As president, I was victorious in the War of 1812. Here's something you may not know about me: as a boy, I was often sick!

I Am...
Horace Mann
1796–1859

education reformer

"A human being is not attaining his full heights until he is educated."

I am the "Father of American public schools." I believed that children should be required to attend publicly funded schools and be taught a wide variety of topics by professional teachers. I served as secretary of the Massachusetts State Board of Education. Here's something you may not know about me: I helped end corporal punishment in schools!

I Am...
John Marshall
1755–1835

chief justice

"The Constitution is color-blind, and neither knows nor tolerates classes among citizens."

I was chief justice of the United States for 34 years. I empowered the judicial branch by formulating *judicial review*—the idea that the Supreme Court can decide if a law is, or is not, in keeping with the Constitution. Here's something you may not know about me: you can still visit my house—it's a museum in Richmond, Virginia!

I Am...
Thurgood Marshall 1908–1993

supreme court justice

"In recognizing the humanity of our fellow beings, we pay ourselves the highest tribute."

I won the *Brown* v. *Board of Education* case, which declared segregation in public schools unconstitutional. Later I became the first African American Supreme Court justice. Here's something you may not know about me: my original name was Thoroughgood, but I changed it in second grade because I didn't like to spell it!

I Am... Cyrus McCormick 1809–1884

inventor

"One step at a time, the hardest one first."

I invented the mechanical reaper in 1831. My invention enabled farmers to harvest as much grain in an hour as what used to take a whole day! Today, I am remembered as the "Father of Modern Agriculture." Here's something you may not know about me: I started inventing farm tools when I was still a teenager!

I Am...
James Monroe
1758–1831

founder

"The best form of government is that which is most likely to prevent the greatest sum of evil."

I was the fifth president of the United States. My Monroe Doctrine stated that the United States would not tolerate European intervention in the Americas. Earlier, I fought in the American Revolution and served as a governor, senator, and secretary of state. Here's something you may not know about me: I was the last president to wear a powdered wig!

I Am... J. P. Morgan 1837–1913

banker

"Go as far as you can see; when you get there, you'll be able to see farther."

I was a banker and financier. By 1901 I was one of the wealthiest men in the world. I made deals with tycoons like Cornelius Vanderbilt, Andrew Carnegie, and John D. Rockefeller. Here's something you may not know about me: because of a disease, my nose was actually purple—but I never let it bother me, or hinder my success!

I Am...
Samuel F. B. Morse
1791–1872

inventor

"What hath God wrought?"

I invented the telegraph. The telegraph was the first device that allowed messages to be quickly transmitted over long distances. It utilized a sound pattern of dots and dashes called Morse Code. Here's something you may not know about me: I loved art, and I painted portraits in college to earn money!

I Am... Annie Oakley
1860–1926

"Keep your eye on the high mark and you will hit it....if you keep on aiming and keep on trying, you'll hit the bull's eye of success."

sharpshooter

I was a sharpshooter and one of the star attractions in Buffalo Bill's Wild West Show. My skill at marksmanship—I could hit a dropped playing card at 90 feet five or six times before it hit the ground—made me the first female superstar. Here's something you may not know about me: I was known as the "Little Sure Shot"—I was just five feet tall!

I Am... Barack Obama
b. 1961

"We are the ones we've been waiting for. We are the change that we seek."

president

I was the first African American president of the United States. Issues that I particularly cared about are the economy, universal health care, and civil rights. I also won the Nobel Peace Prize in 2009. Here's something you may not know about me: in high school, I played on the varsity basketball team!

I Am . . . Sandra Day O'Connor b. 1930

supreme court justice

"The power I exert on the court depends on the power of my arguments, not on my gender."

I was the first female member of the Supreme Court. I am a graduate of Stanford Law School, and I served as a state senator and as a judge in Arizona. President Ronald Reagan appointed me to the Court in 1981. I retired 25 years later, in 2006. Here's something you may not know about me: I was raised on a ranch, and I wanted to be a rancher when I grew up!

I Am... Thomas Paine
1737–1809

founder

"These are the times that try men's souls. The summer soldier and the sunshine patriot will, in this crisis, shrink from the service of their country."

I wrote the famous pamphlet *Common Sense*. Hundreds of thousands of people read it, and many became convinced to support the fight for American independence. Here's something you may not know about me: because I later supported the French Revolution, I was given honorary French citizenship!

I Am... Rosa Parks 1913–2005

civil rights activist

"Each person must live their life as a model for others."

I refused to give up a seat on a segregated bus in 1955. That action led to the Montgomery bus boycott, led by Dr. Martin Luther King, Jr. The boycott brought national attention to the civil rights movement. Here's something you may not know about me: I was awarded the Congressional Gold Medal—and the Presidential Medal of Freedom!

I Am... Frances Perkins 1880-1965

social activist

"Being a woman has only bothered me in climbing trees."

I was the first woman appointed to the president's cabinet, serving as secretary of labor under Franklin D. Roosevelt. I helped establish the minimum wage and overtime laws and Social Security. Here's something you may not know about me: when I married, I kept my maiden name, but I had to go to court to do it!

I Am...
Ronald Reagan
1911–2004

"Democracy is worth dying for, because it's the most deeply honorable form of government ever devised by man."

president

I was the governor of California in the 1960s and 1970s and president during the 1980s. As president, I championed free market economics and took a hard line against the Soviet Union in the Cold War. Here's something you may not know about me: before I went into politics, I was a major movie star who appeared in more than 50 Hollywood films!

I Am...
Sally Ride
b. 1951

"All adventures, especially into new territory, are scary."

astronaut

I was the first female American astronaut. On June 18, 1983, I flew into space on the Space Shuttle *Challenger*. I returned to space the next year. All told, I spent more than 343 hours in space! Here's something you may not know about me: one of my greatest passions is motivating girls and young women to pursue careers in science, math, and technology!

I Am... Jackie Robinson
1919–1972

baseball player

"I'm not concerned with your liking or disliking me...all I ask is that you respect me as a human being."

I was the first African American major league baseball player. In 1947, I joined the Brooklyn Dodgers, and I won Rookie of the Year. (Today, that award is named for me!) I was inducted into the National Baseball Hall of Fame. Here's something you may not know about me: in high school, I starred in baseball...and football, basketball, track and field, and tennis!

I Am...
John D. Rockefeller
1839–1937

"Don't be afraid to give up the good to go for the great."

oil tycoon

I founded the Standard Oil Company and was the first American to make one billion dollars. After I retired, I donated about half of my fortune to charitable organizations. Here's something you may not know about me: as a child, I raised turkeys and sold potatoes to earn money; at my first "real" job, when I was a teenager, I earned 50 cents a day!

71

I Am...
Eleanor Roosevelt
1884–1962

first lady

"Friendship with one's self is all important, because without it one cannot be friends with anyone else...."

I was the first lady for 12 years. I worked to promote greater rights for workers, women, and African Americans. Later, I served as a delegate to the United Nations, and I helped write the Universal Declaration of Human Rights. Here's something you may not know about me: when I was a girl, I was insecure about my looks—but I grew out of it!

72

I Am...
Franklin D. Roosevelt
1882–1945

president

"Democracy cannot succeed unless [citizens] are prepared to choose wisely. The real safeguard of democracy, therefore, is education."

I am the only U.S. president to serve four terms. I led the country through the Great Depression and through most of World War II. My New Deal programs, designed to ease life during the Depression, dramatically increased the role of the federal government. Here's something you may not know about me: my legs were paralyzed, but I didn't let that stop me!

I Am...
Sacagawea
1787(?) – 1812

guide

"Everything I do is for my people."

I served as a guide and interpreter for the Lewis and Clark Expedition. The presence of a woman indicated the party was peaceful. Also, I helped the expedition obtain much needed horses from a band led by my brother. Here's something you may not know about me: my name means "Bird Woman"!

I Am... Dred Scott
1795–1858

plaintiff

"My words was too poor to explain how it feels to be a slave."

I was a slave in Missouri, but I was taken to live for a time where slavery was prohibited. I used that as a basis to sue for my freedom. In 1857's *Dred Scott* v. *Sandford*, the Supreme Court ruled that I was not a citizen and so had no right to sue. Here's something you may not know about me: new owners freed me shortly after I lost my case!

I Am...
Upton Sinclair
1878–1968

author

"You don't have to be satisfied with America as you find it. You can change it."

I won the Pulitzer Prize for fiction. My best-known work is *The Jungle*, a novel that exposed the cruel treatment of immigrant workers and the unsanitary conditions in meat packing factories. Here's something you may not know about me: I worked undercover in Chicago meat packing plants to do research for the book!

I Am... Sitting Bull
1831(?) – 1890

spiritual leader

"I wish it to be remembered that I was the last man of my tribe to surrender my rifle."

My real name was Tatanka Yotanka. I was a Hunkpapa Lakota Sioux leader who inspired Indians to resist white incursion into and settlement on traditional Indian lands. I inspired the victorious fighters at the Battle of Little Bighorn. Here's something you may not know about me: the U.S. Postal Service issued a Great Americans stamp with my picture on it!

I Am... John Smith 1580–1631

leader

"He that will not work shall not eat...for the labors of ...honest and industrious men shall not be consumed by...idle loiterers."

I led the settlers at Jamestown, the first permanent English colony in America. The settlement almost failed, but I made everyone work hard to ensure its survival. Here's something you may not know about me: before coming to Jamestown, I was a soldier who was once captured in battle and sold into slavery!

I Am... Squanto
1585(?) – 1622

guide

"All white men are not bad....Many white men are good."

My real name was Tisquantum. I helped the Pilgrims survive the first winter in the New World. I already knew English because I had been kidnapped and sent to Spain and then England. Here's something you may not know about me: Plymouth was actually built on the site of my former village, which had been destroyed by disease!

I Am...
Elizabeth Cady Stanton
1815–1902

women's rights activist

"We hold these truths to be self-evident: that all men and women are created equal."

With Lucretia Mott, I organized the first women's rights convention, in Seneca Falls, New York, in 1847. My Declaration of Sentiments declared women were equal to men and should be allowed to vote and own property. Here's something you may not know about me: my father was an attorney, and as a girl I loved to read his law books and debate legal ideas!

I Am...
Harriet Beecher Stowe
1811–1896

author

"It's a matter of taking the side of the weak against the strong, something the best people have always done."

I wrote a novel, *Uncle Tom's Cabin*, that portrayed slavery as evil and immoral. The book was published just ten years before the Civil War and heightened tensions in the country. Here's something you may not know about me: when I lived in Connecticut, Mark Twain was my neighbor, and we were friends!

I Am . . .
William Graham Sumner
1840–1910

sociologist

"What we prepare for is what we shall get."

I was a Yale professor who did pioneering work in the study of societies. I coined the word *ethnocentrism*. Ethnocentrism means the tendency of people to judge other peoples' cultures according to the standards of their own culture. Here's something you may not know about me: I was the first person in the United States to teach a course called "sociology"!

I Am... William Howard Taft 1857–1930

president

"A government is for the benefit of all the people."

I was the 27th president of the United States. I used what is called "Dollar Diplomacy" to develop American security and business interests overseas. Later, I served as chief justice of the United States. Here's something you may not know about me: I was both the heaviest president ever elected, and the last to have facial hair!

I Am... Ida Tarbell
1857–1944

journalist

"Imagination is the only key to the future. Without it none exists—with it all things are possible."

I was one of the "muckrakers"—the first investigative journalists. My *History of the Standard Oil Company* exposed the company's unfair business practices. It continues to inspire journalists even today. Here's something you may not know about me: when I attended Allegheny College, there were only four other girls there!

I Am... "Zachary Taylor" 1784–1850

president

"I have always done my duty. I am ready to die. My only regret is for the friends I leave behind me."

I spent 40 years in the U.S. military, fought in three wars, and was the 12th president. My victories in the Mexican War made me a national hero. I died after only 16 months in office. Here's something you may not know about me: as a child on the Kentucky frontier, I lived in a small cabin, and never attended school!

I Am...
Henry David Thoreau
1817–1862

author

"Aim above morality. Be not simply good, be good for something."

I wrote *Walden*, a book praising living simply in natural surroundings. I also wrote "On the Duty of Civil Disobedience," an essay in which I argued that people should refuse to obey laws that they think are unjust. Here's something you may not know about me: my father owned a pencil factory, and I worked there most of my life!

I Am...
Bill Tilden
1893–1953

tennis player

"Never change a winning game; always change a losing one."

I was the most famous tennis player of the 1920s. I could serve a ball at 163 mph! I set many tennis records, some of which still haven't been broken. Because I was so tall, people called me "Big Bill." Here's something you may not know about me: I also wrote and starred in some Broadway plays!

I Am...
Harry S. Truman
1884–1972

president

"If you can't stand the heat, get out of the kitchen."

I was the 33rd president. I was the one who made the decision to drop atomic bombs on Japan. After the war, my foreign policy of opposing the spread of communism was called the Truman Doctrine. Here's something you may not know about me: I once was a partner in a men's clothing store in Kansas City, Missouri!

I Am...
Frederick Jackson Turner
1861–1932

"Each age tries to form its own conception of the past. Each age writes the history of the past anew...."

historian

I was a professor, author, and historian. In my most famous essay, "The Significance of the Frontier in American History," I explained how important the frontier was to the development of America and Americans. Here's something you may not know about me: my father was a local historian, and he helped me get interested in history!

I Am... Mark Twain
1835–1910

"A man cannot be comfortable without his own approval."

author

I wrote *The Adventures of Tom Sawyer, Adventures of Huckleberry Finn,* and many other books. They are entertaining yet serious explorations of moral issues. My real name was Samuel Clemens. Here's something you may not know about me: I was a riverboat pilot, and "mark twain" is a riverboat term that means the depth of the water is a safe 12 feet!

I Am...
Cornelius Vanderbilt
1794–1877

"If I had learned education I would not have had time to learn anything else."

entrepreneur

I was one of the richest Americans who ever lived. I made my fortune through the steamship business and, later, railroads. Because of my shipping business, people called me "Commodore," which is the highest rank in the navy. Here's something you may not know about me: I started working on ferries and steamboats when I was only 11 years old!

I Am . . . Amerigo Vespucci

1451(?) – 1512

explorer

"There is here, as in all countries, advantages and disadvantages."

I was an early explorer of South America. A German mapmaker, after reading my letters describing the New World, put a version of my name on his map, and that's where the name *America* comes from! Here's something you may not know about me: I was among the first Europeans to see the Amazon River!

I Am... George Washington 1732–1799

father of the country

"I have no other view than to promote the public good."

I was the Commander-in-Chief of the Continental Army and the first president of the United States. Today, I am revered as the "Father of the Country." My home at Mount Vernon, outside of Washington, D.C., is visited by people from all over the world. Here's something you may not know about me: as a teenager, I worked as a surveyor!

I Am...
Booker T. Washington
1856–1915

educator

"I will permit no man to narrow and degrade my soul by making me hate him."

I was born into slavery, but grew up to found the Tuskegee Normal and Industrial Institute, a vocational school for African Americans. I was an outspoken leader for economic opportunities for African Americans. Here's something you may not know about me: my book, *Up From Slavery*, earned me an invitation to visit President Theodore Roosevelt!

I Am... Eli Whitney
1765–1825

"One of my primary objects is to form the tools so the tools themselves shall fashion the work...."

inventor

I invented the cotton gin! The cotton gin separated the seeds from the fibers. This made cotton more profitable, and strengthened the South. I also promoted the use of interchangeable, or standardized, parts in manufacturing. Here's something you may not know about me: I started a business making nails when I was only 14 years old!

I Am... Walt Whitman
1819–1892

poet

"Keep your face always toward the sunshine—and shadows will fall behind you."

I was one of the most important American poets. My collection of poems *Leaves of Grass* is a classic of American literature. My poems celebrate life, democracy, and the United States. Here's something you may not know about me: I actually got fired from one job just because my boss didn't like my poetry!

96

I Am... Woodrow Wilson

1856–1924

president

"America was established not to create wealth but to...discover and maintain liberty among men."

I was president of the United States during World War I. After the war, I was the chief planner of the League of Nations, for which I won the Nobel Peace Prize. Earlier, I had served as president of Princeton University and governor of New Jersey. Here's something you may not know about me: the Civil War prevented me from starting school until I was nine!

I Am...
Orville Wright
1871–1948

"We were lucky enough to grow up in an environment where there was always much encouragement...."

aviator

I am the world's first airplane pilot! My brother Wilbur and I built the first airplane. In 1903, it flew for the first time at Kitty Hawk, North Carolina. We had a coin toss to see who would fly first, and I won! Here's something you may not know about me: my interest in flying was sparked by a flying toy my father brought home for my brother and me!

I Am...
Wilbur Wright
1867–1912

aviator

"It is possible to fly without motors, but not without knowledge and skill."

My brother Orville and I built the first airplane. In 1903, he made the first airplane flight at Kitty Hawk, North Carolina. I made the second flight! Here's something you may not know about me: as a teenager, my front teeth were knocked out in an ice-skating accident, and for a long time I was very self-conscious about my looks!

I Am... Brigham Young
1801–1877

"Don't try to tear down other people's religion....Build up your own...and invite your listeners to enter in and enjoy its glories."

religious leader

I was the second president of the Church of Jesus Christ of Latter-Day Saints (Mormon Church). I led my followers 1,300 miles from Illinois to Utah to find a place we could freely practice our religion. Here's something you may not know about me: as a young man, I worked as a blacksmith and as a carpenter!

Made in the USA
San Bernardino, CA
16 April 2016